Cat's Lunch

HOUGHTON MIFFLIN   BOSTON

Cat cooks lunch.

Cat makes a mess.

Hen, Duck, and Fox clean
the pans.

Cat's friends pat him
on the back.
"Thanks for lunch!"
they say.

Fox Helps Hen

HOUGHTON MIFFLIN   BOSTON

Hen tells Fox, "Please put
strawberries on the cake."

Fox eats a strawberry.

Fox eats all the strawberries.

3

Hen tells Fox, "Please get
more strawberries!"